# Queens and Princesses

VITHDRAWN

# Nefertiti

## OF EGYPT

*by Mary Englar*

**Consultant:**
Leo Depuydt, Professor
Department of Egyptology and Ancient Western Asian Studies
Brown University
Providence, Rhode Island

Capstone press
Mankato, Minnesota

Snap Books are published by Capstone Press,
151 Good Counsel Drive, P.O. Box 669, Mankato, Minnesota 56002.
www.capstonepress.com

*Library of Congress Cataloging-in-Publication Data*
Englar, Mary.
    Nefertiti of Egypt / by Mary Englar.
    p. cm. — (Snap books. Queens and princesses)
    Summary: "Describes the life of Nefertiti of Egypt" — Provided by publisher.
    Includes bibliographical references and index.
    ISBN-13: 978-1-4296-2309-4 (hardcover)
    ISBN-10: 1-4296-2309-8 (hardcover)
    1. Nefertiti, Queen of Egypt, 14th cent. B.C. — Juvenile literature. 2. Queens
— Egypt — Biography — Juvenile literature. 3. Egypt — History — Eighteenth
dynasty, ca. 1570-1320 B.C. — Juvenile literature. I. Title.
DT87.45.E64 2009
932'.014092 — dc22                                                    2008027662

**Editor:** Megan Peterson
**Book Designer:** Bobbi J. Wyss
**Set Designer:** Juliette Peters
**Photo Researcher:** Wanda Winch

**Photo Credits:**
Art Resource, N.Y./ Bildarchiv Preussischer Kulturbesitz, 23; Art Resource, N.Y./ Erich Lessing, 6, 9; Art
Resource, N.Y./ François Guenet, 18; Art Resource, N.Y./ Réunion des Musées Nationaux, 11; Art Resource,
N.Y./ Scala, 12, 19; Dreamstime/Kharidehal Abhirama Ashwin, 27; Getty Images Inc./The Bridgeman Art
Library, 13, 24; Getty Images Inc./Robert Harding World Imagery, 25; The Image Works/SSPL, 17; Mary
Evans Picture Library, cover, 21; North Wind Picture Archives, 16; Shutterstock/Kharidehal Abhirama
Ashwin, 7; Shutterstock/Mario Bruno, 15, 29; Shutterstock/Oleg_Z, 5

Essential content terms are **bold** and are defined at the bottom of the page where
they first appear.

1  2  3  4  5  6  14  13  12  11  10  09

# Table of Contents

# THE *Great* RECEPTION

King Amenhotep IV and Queen Nefertiti of the ancient Egyptian **empire** prepared to celebrate the 12th year of his rule. They spent hours preparing for this great event. The royal couple dressed alike in white linen robes with red sashes. Gold jewelry sparkled on their arms, ears, ankles, and necks.

The king and queen climbed aboard their golden carrying chair. The heavy chair took 15 strong men to lift. Servants ran beside the chair. They waved fans to cool the couple under the hot desert sun. Egyptians lined the royal road to cheer for their king and queen. The royal couple rode to the outdoor celebration on the south side of Akhetaten, the royal city.

When they arrived, Amenhotep IV and Nefertiti climbed onto a high platform. They sat on golden thrones and gazed out at their subjects. Their six daughters played behind them. The air was thick with perfume. Representatives from neighboring kingdoms stood in a long line. They wanted to pay **tribute** to the powerful king. Amenhotep IV asked the kingdoms he ruled to honor him. The kingdoms of Libya, Nubia, Punt, and Syria-Palestine were happy to obey.

First, the representatives bowed to the ground. They presented Amenhotep IV with animal skins, chariots, horses, weapons, perfumes, spices, and sacks of gold. Leopards, antelopes, monkeys, and even a lion were among the many gifts.

empire — a large territory ruled by a powerful leader
tribute — gifts given to a king to show respect

As queen, Nefertiti was the most famous woman in ancient Egypt.

5

When the ceremony ended, the king and queen gave gold to their servants for planning the big event. Then they returned to the palace for a grand dinner. The smell of roasted meat filled the air. Guests feasted on whole ducks and grilled beef. Mountains of grapes, figs, pomegranates, and dates were ripe for the taking. Servants carried trays heaped with cakes, onions, lettuce, and cucumbers. Servants poured water on the king's and queen's hands when they were finished eating.

Musicians played flutes, harps, tambourines, and drums. They sang songs that all Egyptians knew by heart. Dancers leapt like acrobats before the musicians. People clapped along to the music and danced far into the night.

Nefertiti and Amenhotep IV had much to celebrate. It was around the year 1340 BC, and they ruled the largest and richest empire in the world. To honor the king and queen, artists carved the historic celebration in tombs surrounding the royal city. Still, historians know very little about this mysterious couple. Everything they know comes from **artifacts**, paintings, and **hieroglyphs** carved into the royal tombs at Akhetaten.

Artists carved these Egyptian harpists in a temple at Thebes, the religious capital of ancient Egypt.

artifact — an object used in the past that was made by people
hieroglyph — a picture or symbol used in the ancient Egyptian system of writing

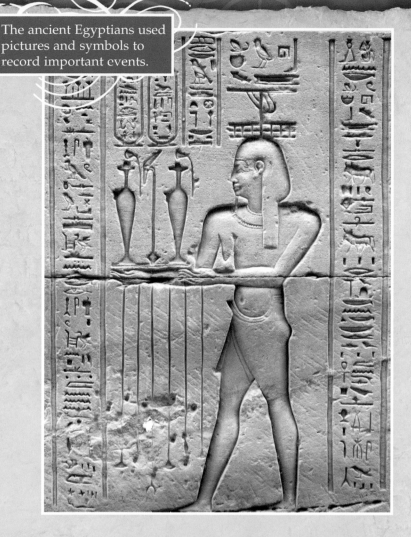

The ancient Egyptians used pictures and symbols to record important events.

# EGYPTIAN HIEROGLYPHS

Egyptian hieroglyphs are one of the oldest writing systems in the world. Ancient Egyptians called the writing "words of the gods." The language used more than 700 pictures and symbols. Ancient Egyptian students studied for many years to master the writing. They carved or wrote the language on tombs, temples, and scrolls made from papyrus reeds.

Until the early 1800s, no one understood how to read the language. In 1822, a Frenchman named Jean Francois Champollion cracked the system. That year, he correctly read the names of many past Egyptian kings.

# CHILDHOOD IN
# *Ancient Egypt*

# 2

Nefertiti's childhood is a mystery. Very few facts are known about her family. Historians believe she was born around 1364 BC at Thebes, the capital of ancient Egypt. Many historians agree she was the daughter of Ay. Ay was an adviser to Amenhotep IV's father, King Amenhotep III. Ay was also the brother of Amenhotep IV's mother, Queen Tiy.

A painting from Ay's tomb offers one clue about Nefertiti's childhood. The painting shows Ay and his wife, Tey, receiving gold necklaces from Queen Nefertiti and King Amenhotep IV. The painting describes Tey as Nefertiti's nurse. Tey was not Nefertiti's mother, but it's believed she raised her from a young age. Some historians believe Nefertiti might have been Ay's child from a first marriage.

Historians discovered another clue in paintings that show Nefertiti with a younger sister, Mutnodjmet. Mutnodjmet appeared in many paintings with Nefertiti's daughters. She also appeared on the walls of Ay's tomb. Some historians believe the sisters were nieces of Queen Tiy.

Ay (left) and Tey (right) received gold necklaces from King Amenhotep IV and Queen Nefertiti.

# KING AMENHOTEP III

At the time Nefertiti was born, King Amenhotep III had ruled Egypt for more than 20 years. He was very wealthy. Leaders from neighboring kingdoms believed that Amenhotep III had unlimited amounts of gold. Kingdoms he conquered gave expensive gifts as payment for his protection. These payments were called tribute. Leaders from Nubia, a kingdom south of Egypt, brought him sacks of gold.

The ancient Egyptians lived along the banks of the Nile River. The river flooded nearly every year. The floodwaters carried good soil for farming. Farmers planted their crops in the rich, black soil. The Nile also provided water for their farms.

The Egyptians depended on the Nile River flood for most of their food. When the harvest was good, the people lived well. When the Nile did not flood, the people of Egypt starved. Under Amenhotep III, harvests were good, and the kingdom was peaceful.

# FAMILY LIFE

Most ancient Egyptians loved children and wanted large families. But life in ancient Egypt was hard for everyone. Many babies and young children died from disease or accidents. Nefertiti's parents made **amulets** to protect her. These small pieces of jewelry represented the gods or sacred animals. They were made from gemstones, metal, shells, seeds, bones, and flowers. Red amulets were believed to protect children from danger. Most Egyptians preferred blue-green amulets because they represented life and good health.

Like all Egyptian children, Nefertiti did not wear clothing except for special occasions. She also had a shaved head except for one lock of hair. Around the age of 12, her sidelock was shaved off. All Egyptian children wore their hair in this special style.

As a young girl, Nefertiti had a shaved head except for one sidelock of hair, as shown on this statue.

Like most ancient Egyptian children, Nefertiti loved games and toys. Historians have found puppets, rattles, tops, and animals with moving jaws and tails. Some children had dolls with real hair, clothing, and tiny furniture.

Many ancient Egyptian families had cats. Cats were sometimes worshipped as gods. Bastet was a goddess of love and fertility. She had the head of a cat and the body of a woman. When a cat died, it was often mummified and placed in its own tomb. The punishment for killing a cat was death.

Many ancient Egyptian children played with dolls. Some of the dolls had real hair.

## EDUCATION

Only a few ancient Egyptians knew how to read and write. Poor children did not go to school. Boys learned their fathers' jobs. Girls learned how to cook and sew. Wealthy boys and girls, like Nefertiti, were educated in a palace or had tutors. They studied math, writing, and reading.

## THE BEAUTIFUL WOMAN HAS COME

King Amenhotep III ruled Egypt for almost 40 years. When he died, his eldest son, Amenhotep IV, became king. Amenhotep IV needed a wife. He looked for a strong girl from a noble family. Amenhotep IV chose Nefertiti, whose name means "the beautiful woman has come."

Amenhotep IV became king of Egypt when his father died.

13

# 3

# QUEEN
# *Nefertiti*

Around 1352 BC, Nefertiti married King Amenhotep IV. No written histories mention Nefertiti until she became the king's wife. Most girls in ancient Egypt married young. Historians believe Nefertiti was about 12 years old when she became queen. Amenhotep IV was around the same age.

Amenhotep IV was not raised to be king. His older brother, Prince Thutmose, was groomed to be Egypt's next ruler. But when Thutmose died, Amenhotep IV became next in line to be king. Amenhotep IV was not prepared to rule when he took the throne. At first, his mother ruled alongside him. Many foreign leaders sent important letters to Queen Tiy instead of the young king.

Nefertiti became queen of Egypt when she married King Amenhotep IV in 1352 BC.

Many Egyptian men and women wore wigs. Nefertiti shaved her head with a bronze razor to make her wigs fit better. Her wigs were made of human hair. They were cut short in the back and longer near her face. The wigs left her neck bare in the back, which kept her cool. Soon all the royal women began to wear this wig style.

Nefertiti had crowns made in many styles and colors. When she first became queen, Nefertiti wore crowns with tall feathers, cow horns, and sun discs. These crowns honored Hathor, goddess of the sky. Later, Nefertiti's favorite was a tall blue flat-topped crown. This crown looked similar to her husband's war crown. A gold band held her crown in place. Each of her crowns had a metal cobra on the front. The cobra was an Egyptian symbol of royalty. Only the king and queen could wear it.

The queen's clothing was made of the finest linen. The material was so thin that her skin showed through it. She usually wore a white robe embroidered with gold. Plants were used to dye fabrics yellow, red, and blue. She tied her robes at the waist with colorful sashes. Nefertiti owned many gold earrings, necklaces, armbands, and ankle bracelets. Some were also made with colored beads and precious stones such as turquoise.

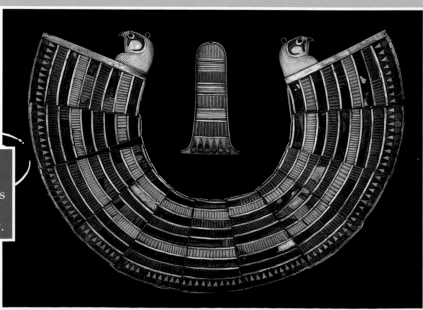

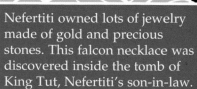
Nefertiti owned lots of jewelry made of gold and precious stones. This falcon necklace was discovered inside the tomb of King Tut, Nefertiti's son-in-law.

Nefertiti and her family worshipped Aten, a sun god.

## A NEW RELIGION

For hundreds of years, the ancient Egyptians worshipped many gods. They believed that the king was also a god. Only the king could ask the gods for good harvests. Priests oversaw the many temples. They bathed, perfumed, and clothed statues of the gods. Ordinary people rarely saw the gods and goddesses housed in the temples. Most people worshipped at home.

Early in his rule, King Amenhotep IV changed his religious beliefs. He believed that the Aten, a minor sun god, was the most important god. Painted or carved as the sun's disc, Aten gave light and life to the earth. Amenhotep IV built new temples at Thebes to worship Aten. He ignored tradition and encouraged Nefertiti to worship in the new temples.

Most of the temple paintings at Thebes show Nefertiti alone or with her small daughters as she worshipped Aten. In one temple, Nefertiti is shown acting as Aten's high priest. Nefertiti's new religious duties gave her more power than most previous Egyptian queens.

# BUILDING A
## *New City*

About four years after Nefertiti became queen, her husband decided to leave the religious capital of Thebes. He wanted to build a new city to honor his chosen god, Aten. He also wanted to replace all of the old gods with Aten. The priests were soon dismissed.

### THE CITY OF AKHETATEN

The king chose an empty plain along the Nile for his new city. He named the new city for Aten. Akhetaten means "horizon of Aten." Akhetaten was halfway between Thebes and the capital of Lower Egypt, Memphis. Limestone cliffs protected the city.

The king and queen also changed their names to honor Aten. Amenhotep IV changed his name to Akhenaten, which means "living spirit of Aten." Nefertiti became Neferneferuaten, which means "beautiful are the beauties of Aten."

The royal couple designed the new city. Along a wide road, builders quickly put up new palaces, temples, government offices, and houses. After about a year of construction, Nefertiti and her growing family took a royal boat down the Nile. Soon, the city of Akhetaten rose from the desert like a glistening jewel. Chariots carried the royal family to the main palace. As many as 50,000 Egyptians moved to Akhetaten to serve the king and queen in their new city.

Queen Nefertiti and King Akhenaten changed the religion of ancient Egypt.

# THE ROYAL PALACES

Nefertiti and her husband brought the best builders and artists to Akhetaten. They built a total of four palaces in the new city. The family traveled between their palaces by chariot. Palace walls were painted with colorful scenes from their lives. The murals showed the royal couple and their daughters relaxing on floor cushions. The tiled floors were covered with scenes of the Nile, flowers, fish, and ducks.

Flowers and fruit trees filled the palace gardens. Many gardens extended down to the Nile's edge. Pools with fish and lotus plants shone brightly in the hot sun. One of the palaces had a zoo. The zoo housed cattle, gazelles, wild goats, and at least one lion. Nefertiti's daughters played with the baby gazelles.

# A LOVING FAMILY

The art of Akhetaten was very personal. Before this time, Egyptian artists painted or carved pictures of the king and queen only on formal occasions. Nearly every house in Akhetaten had a sculpture or a painting of Nefertiti and her family. Artists painted tomb walls with events from the royal couple's life. They showed Nefertiti and her family as they relaxed, ate, and worshipped together. Nefertiti's six daughters crawled on her lap and touched her face. In every image, Aten's rays reached down with tiny hands to give them the gift of life.

This carving shows Nefertiti (right) and Akhenaten (left) spending time with three of their six daughters.

Statues, paintings, and carvings show Nefertiti and Akhenaten as a loving couple.

## BELOVED CHIEF WIFE

Images of Nefertiti with her husband show that they were very close. They held hands during ceremonies. Nefertiti kissed Akhenaten as she put on his necklace. Akhenaten described Nefertiti as the "Chief Wife of the King, his beloved." He also described her as "sweet of love" and "possessed of charm."

Some of these names were traditional for Egypt's queens. The number of titles he gave Nefertiti is unusual. Akhenaten really loved his beautiful queen and partner. In ancient Egypt, it was common for kings to have many wives. Akhenaten honored Nefertiti with the title of "Chief Wife."

Queen Nefertiti was also a strong leader. She drove her own chariot down the royal road. She was honored with statues as big as her husband's. She was even shown killing Egypt's enemies, just as the king did.

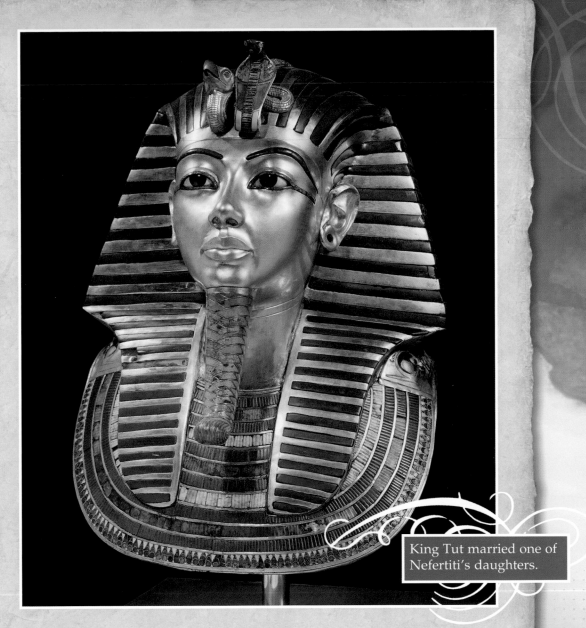

King Tut married one of Nefertiti's daughters.

## KING TUT

One of the most famous kings of Egypt, Tutankhamen, was born at Akhetaten. Historians believe he was the son of King Akhenaten and a secondary wife. Nine-year-old Tut became king when Akhenaten died. He married one of Nefertiti's daughters and soon moved the capital back to Thebes. Unlike his father, King Tut returned to Egypt's traditional religion.

# A Mysterious End

For the first 12 years of her married life, Nefertiti was shown as happy with her husband and daughters. Life in Akhetaten was good. They had plenty of food, many palaces, and the riches of the Egyptian empire. Akhetaten was far from the traditional Egyptian capitals. Nefertiti and Akhenaten seemed to ignore life beyond their city.

## NEFERTITI DISAPPEARS

Nefertiti disappeared from record sometime after the 12th-year celebration. Queen Tiy and some of the children also disappeared from the paintings. Historians believe they died. A plague hit the Middle East at that time. The disease possibly spread to the royal city.

Around this same time, artists carved King Akhenaten with a new king, Smenkhkare. Some historians argue that Nefertiti was in fact the new king. They believe she changed her name and became co-ruler of ancient Egypt. There are no records to solve the mystery. Nefertiti's tomb has never been found. Historians do not know when she died or where she was buried.

Nefertiti's death remains a mystery to this day.

## A BEAUTIFUL DISCOVERY

In 1912, German historian Ludwig Borchardt dug for artifacts in Akhetaten, now known as Amarna. By chance, workers uncovered the workshop of the city's most famous artist, Thutmose. They found many beautiful sculptures buried in the sand and rubble.

The most important discovery was a life-sized bust of Queen Nefertiti. The limestone bust had fallen off a shelf and landed upside down in the sand. For more than 3,000 years the bust remained untouched. Workers were surprised to find it had very little damage. Historians recognized Nefertiti's blue flat-topped crown and regal face.

## DISCOVERY OF AKHETATEN

The first European to document the ruins of Akhetaten was the Frenchman Edmé Jomard. In 1799, he mapped the remains of walls, a huge gate, and the royal road at a place called Amarna. Later explorers translated the names found on tomb walls and border markers as King Akhenaten and Queen Nefertiti.

The kings after Akhenaten erased the names and faces from his monuments. Historians believe that later kings were angry with Akhenaten for changing the religion of Egypt. Historians have spent many years trying to understand the story of the Amarna ruins.

Many stories surround how Nefertiti's bust left Egypt. For some reason, Egyptian officials did not claim the bust. Borchardt took it back to Germany. Some think he smuggled it out of Egypt, but no one knows for sure.

In 1924, the New Museum in Berlin, Germany, put Nefertiti's bust on display for the first time. Visitors admired her beauty. The bust soon became the museum's most popular exhibit. Today the bust is still on display in Berlin. Nefertiti's natural beauty and the artistic quality have made it one of the most famous works of Egyptian art.

## A LASTING LEGACY

More than 3,000 years ago, Queen Nefertiti ruled alongside one of the most powerful kings in the ancient world. She helped create a new city and a new religion. She also loved and cared for her husband and six daughters. Nefertiti remains a symbol of the rich culture of ancient Egypt.

Historians believe Nefertiti's famous limestone bust was a model for future works of art.

# Glossary

**amulet** (AM-yoo-let) — a small charm believed to protect the wearer from harm

**ancient** (AYN-shunt) — from a long time ago

**artifact** (AR-tuh-fakt) — an object used in the past that was made by people

**bust** (BUHST) — a sculpture of a person's head and shoulders

**chariot** (CHAYR-ee-uht) — a light, two-wheeled cart pulled by horses

**empire** (EM-pyr) — a large territory ruled by a powerful leader

**hieroglyph** (HYE-ruh-glif) — a picture or symbol used in the ancient Egyptian system of writing

**ore** (OR) — a metal found in rock; the ancient Egyptians created different types of makeup from crushed ore mixed with oils or animal fat.

**plague** (PLAYG) — a disease that spreads quickly and kills most people who catch it

**pomegranate** (POM-uh-gran-it) — a round, reddish-yellow fruit

**tomb** (TOOM) — a grave, room, or building used to hold a dead body

**tribute** (TRIB-yoot) — gifts given to a king to show respect

# Read More

**Lange, Brenda.** *Nefertiti.* Ancient World Leaders. New York: Chelsea House, 2008.

**Rubalcaba, Jill.** *National Geographic Investigates Ancient Egypt: Archaeology Unlocks the Secrets of Egypt's Past.* National Geographic Investigates. Washington, D.C.: National Geographic, 2007.

**Tyldesley, Joyce.** *Egypt.* Insiders. New York: Simon & Schuster Books for Young Readers, 2007.

# Internet Sites

FactHound offers a safe, fun way to find educator-approved Internet sites related to this book.

Here's what you do:

1. Visit *www.facthound.com*
2. Choose your grade level.
3. Begin your search.

This book's ID number is 9781429623094.

FactHound will fetch the best sites for you!

# Index